Redesigning our homes
is a powerful way of reconceiving,
redefining and expressing who we are,
or who we are becoming.

ALTAR  YOUR SPACE

ALTAR YOUR SPACE

A GUIDE TO THE RESTORATIVE HOME

JAGATJOTI S. KHALSA

FOREWORD BY JOELY FISHER

PHOTOGRAPHY BY MIKE GOEDECKE &
JAGATJOTI S. KHALSA

MANDALA
PUBLISHING
SAN RAFAEL, CA

MANDALA
PUBLISHING

17 Paul Drive
San Rafael, CA 94903

415.526.1370
Fax: 415.526.1394
www.mandala.org

Library of Congress Cataloging-in-Publication Data available.

ISBN-10: 1-60109-008-0
ISBN-13: 978-1-60109-008-9

www.altaryourspace.com

ROOTS of PEACE   REPLANTED PAPER

Palace Press International, in association with Roots of Peace, will plant two trees for
each tree used in the manufacturing of this book. Roots of Peace is an internationally
renowned humanitarian organization dedicated to eradicating land mines worldwide
and converting war-torn lands into productive farms and wildlife habitats. Together,
we will plant two million fruit and nut trees in Afghanistan and provide farmers there
with the skills and support necessary for sustainable land use.

10 9 8 7 6 5 4 3 2 1

Printed in Hong Kong by Palace Press International
www.palacepresss.com

CONTENTS

EPIGRAPH

ON ONE OF THEIR LENGTHY WALKING pilgrimages across India, Guru Nanak, founder of Sikhism, and his companion Mardana came to a village notorious for its phony saints, who made their living off of gullible worshippers.

Rather than enter the village, Guru Nanak and Mardana sat down under a jasmine tree and began to meditate in blissful silence. When the spiritual con men in the village learned that Guru Nanak was just outside their town, they became worried that he might enter and deprive them of their living. So they sent an emissary on horseback to meet him. The emissary presented Guru Nanak with a "gift" of a bowl of milk filled completely to the brim. This symbolic message said, in essence, *"There's no room for you in our village. We're full up. We have everything we need. You can move along. You are not welcome here."*

Guru Nanak slowly raised his hand, plucked a jasmine flower from the branch above him and set it gently in the bowl of milk. There it floated serenely on top, without spilling a drop, symbolizing that no matter how full our worldly life appears to be, there is always room for God.

FOREWORD

I WAS RAISED A CATHOLIC CHILD, so for better or for worse, the sounds of tinkling bells and Gregorian chants and the smell of incense catapult me back to a state of reverence. (Also to a state of guilt and restriction...but in a good way.) I can still recall the wooden pew beneath my kilt-clad bottom, the unfolding of the clunky kneeler, always knowing the appropriate times to sit, stand or kneel. It is within the walls of churches, synagogues, temples and mosques that the inhabitants of our planet have always found comfort, tradition, companionship, community and solace.

I suppose that my penchant for trying to recreate those emotions comes from a lifelong search for meaning. I have traveled the globe, sought out teachers, auditioned several belief systems, given up eating meat for nearly thirty years and finally found a way to solve my existential crisis: decorating! In my childhood bedroom I decided to rip off the canopy of my frilly bed so dreams could get in—I was a spiritual, emotional and disturbed child but a hell of a designer. I would seek out antique stores when I was on the road with my mother, Connie Stevens, the consummate entertainer. As an adult, my first home was at the top of the Hollywood Hills, with a great view of everything. Never mind that it was a little prefab foreclosure—I trans-formed it into a villa somewhere in the south of someplace. You might even say that I used it to ensnare my first husband (and I say first only because my father is Eddie Fisher).

So you can imagine the magnetic force with which I was sucked into a place called Tara Home Sacred Interiors. It was like I had found my Holy Grail and out of the corner walked the messiah. Imagine, if you will, walking along Main Street with the undeniable smell of nag champa and the sound of Krishna Das wafting toward you. And then: a veritable lounge on the side-walk, in case you need to rest before taking in the rest—or perhaps

you'll just decide to purchase the outdoor showroom, which is, of course, owner Jagatjoti Khalsa's plan. After your outdoor multi-sensory overload, if you dare to step through the looking glass, you find yourself in a truly intoxicating, magical space. The 5,000 square feet are filled floor to rafter with wood and stone and textiles that make my heart thunder. Once inside you face the lovely dichotomy of the musk and mystery on the one hand, and the affable and jovial Jagatjoti on the other. His turban du jour is purple and he wears it like a crown, if a bit askew. Today, years after our first meeting, Jagatjoti and his family have become part of my life. I feel so lucky to be able to call this man, with his winning sense of humor and keen sense of the spiritual, my friend.

My own "altered space" encompasses my hillside home. It includes the Chinese wedding bed, the Tibetan sex den (a cabana we designed in India that sits next to our pool), a daybed that could sleep the Jolie-Pitt family and a studio that allows me to sneak away from the set and "zen" out.

What a delicious treat that the planet will have this gorgeous book to view the travels and trade secrets of this self-proclaimed "simple shop-keeper." Perhaps someday the trip we've planned with our families to travel the world reinventing all of your homes will come to fruition. For now we will have the pages of *Altar Your Space* with which to journey through Jagatjoti's world, and maybe *altar* our own just a little bit. Jump on the magic carpet and go for the ride.

PEACE AND BLESSINGS
JOELY FISHER

Your greatness is measured by
your gifts, not your possessions.

—YOGI BHAJAN

INTRODUCTION

I STILL RECALL MY FIRST MEETING, over two decades ago, with my spiritual teacher, Yogi Bhajan. In that powerful encounter, I felt I was, at once, in the presence of my teacher, my destiny, my future and my Self. Over the years, he would teach me to serve and uplift others without ego, judgment or attachment, and never to waste one morsel of the grace of God and guru.

Even in that first meeting, in his presence I felt his love and devotion for my soul, and his healing energy and sacred intention. At one point he asked me in his thick Punjabi accent, "Do you know the sacred secret of success in this lifetime?"

I offered several excellent answers to his question: the remembrance of God, the repetition of mantra, good hygiene and such. When I finished, he looked at me and said, "Son, be the altar, not the alternative." And again he repeated, "Be the altar, not the alternative."

I felt the perfection and completeness of his words. Over time, I have savored and contemplated this simple statement, and it has had a deep and lasting impact on me.

What does it mean? What does it mean to you? Its meaning deepens for me over time, as it evolves and gains more traction in my heart. Much of its meaning is embedded in the pages of this book, in the text, the photographs and the designs.

For me, being the altar, not the alternative, means being, living, acting and projecting from a point of neutrality and awareness, wholeness and transcendence. It is about experiencing everything, appreciating all perspectives, being connected to what is before you, without attachment to any one thing or point of view. To me, the altar is a symbol of this very place, your own center and Self, where you find peace, balance, harmony and grace amid the dueling polarities of life.

When you live your life as the altar, not the alternative, you will live a life that is, in the words of my teacher, "happy, healthy and holy," and each day will be rich with the blessings of life, of your soul, of God. Each breath will restore and replenish you. Each action will emerge from a state of consciousness that is balanced, neutral and aware, and from a heart that is prayerful, graceful and grateful.

Altar Your Space is about applying these perspectives to your life, starting with your home environment. It is about designing a sacred living space that embodies the architecture of your soul and connects your consciousness to infinity; that uplifts your spirit; keeps you holy minded; embraces and supports the fullness of your worldly life; and emanates the energy, atmosphere and fragrance of what we call sacred. It is about making your home the altar, not the alternative.

What do you want to experience and feel in your home—beauty, calmness, grace, radiance, joy? What do you want your home to enhance in your life and provide for you and your family—stability, prosperity, opportunity, creativity, spirituality? An "altared" home is a sanctuary for the body, heart and soul of you and your family.

In your essence, you are already whole, complete and perfect, and you can create a living environment that reflects and supports this. It is your birthright to be surrounded by beauty, to know peace and joy, to live royally and happily in a sacred home that elevates your life, uplifts your spirit, restores your soul and connects you with the flow of love and prosperity of the universe.

Without going out of my door,
I can know all things on earth.
Without looking out of my window,
I can know the ways of
heaven.

—FROM "THE INNER LIGHT," BY GEORGE HARRISON

LET'S BEGIN OUR JOURNEY TOGETHER

I AM A LOVER OF THE SACRED AND A DESIGNER OF "ALTARED SPACES." I serve people by assisting them in designing sacred living environments in their own homes. I help them discover a vision of home that lives in their spirit, a vision that is beautiful, elegant, uplifting, practical, functional, comfortable and perfect for them. Then I help them project their vision into their living environment. I help them create a home that supports, nurtures and inspires, a home that reflects who they are, while serving their unique needs.

In helping people design their homes, I don't impose my vision and sensibility on them or their environment. To impose or insinuate my design ideas into others' homes would rob them of the most exciting possible relationship with their homes. Those houses are not my house; I'm not going to live in them. I don't choose others' goals for them. I assist them in their process. Their goal, their vision of how they want their home to look and feel, must come from within. And when they truly accomplish their goal of designing their home as an altared space, they often feel better in their home than they ever have before. They feel at home in the deepest possible way. They even feel better about themselves. That's how we ought to feel, and how it's possible to feel, in our own homes.

Creating a sacred home environment isn't a matter of aesthetics; of throwing money at our homes; of filling them with elegant, stylish or expensive items according to classical or modern design theories. That's the kind of home I grew up in. Every room was perfectly designed—for a magazine shoot—but not necessarily for living in.

When I was twelve, my house was featured in an upscale magazine. And it looked beautiful in the magazine! It was an artificially elegant environment, designed and set up to photograph well and impress magazine readers. It was picture perfect! It just wasn't a home I felt completely at home in.

There were rooms in my home that I never went into. To me they felt sterile and uninviting. They were designed aesthetically but without taking me into account. I felt uncomfortable in them, as if I didn't belong. There was no place for me to be me. The only places in my home where I felt at home, and where I spent significant time, were my bedroom, the playroom in the basement and the kitchen. The rest of the house was mostly space I passed either through or by.

Many years later I had the opportunity to spend time in a wide variety of altared spaces. I visited and worshipped in mosques,

churches, gurdwaras (Sikh temples), other temples and powerful nature sites. I also discovered that some of the most powerful altared and sacred spaces were in private homes. And I learned the difference between the beautiful, the elegant, the spectacular, the well-designed—and the sacred. An altared space can embody all of the four qualities mentioned above, but those qualities do not in themselves constitute the sacred, just as the stylish magazine photo shoot of my childhood home was not a visual record of a sacred home but rather a designer's palate.

Take one moment here to think about the different homes you've spent time in, whether of friends, family or acquaintances. Which one of these homes feels the best, the warmest, the calmest, the most comfortable, the one where time seems to pass in relaxed enjoyment? Now, is the home you picked the one with the most expensive decor, the home with the most spectacular stuff? I've done this little exercise myself, and the answer to the above question was a definitive no! There's something else, something almost intangible and indefinable, in the homes where we feel the most comfortable, peaceful and at home. Money, artistry and impressive things do not, in themselves, make a sacred space.

Designing an altared space in your home—choosing and arranging the varied elements around you in a way that is pleasing, harmonious and comfortable—is like creating a work of art or solving and piecing together a beautiful puzzle where you will live. It is not about filling, enhancing or even transforming your space. It is about creating a place where you feel completely nourished and at home on every level, in every part, from your front entrance, through the halls and stairways and the open rooms—living room, dining room, kitchen— all the way to your bedroom, the inner sanctum of your "temple."

In a sacred home environment, your restoration should begin as you approach your front door. Each area of your home, and all of its various elements, should have a pleasing, comforting, healing or enlivening effect on your consciousness and on your subconscious. Statues, furniture, carpeting, objects, lighting, flowers, paint color, pictures and paintings, the sounds of soft music or fountain water—all should be consciously placed throughout your home in a harmonious mosaic designed to lead you deeper into an environment of soothing beauty and of physical, emotional and spiritual restoration.

Experience has shown me that with a little help and guidance, a little reflection and imagination, anyone can design any space to serve any purpose and invoke any feeling that he or she desires. You don't have to hire a professional designer or a feng shui expert to tell you whether or not your house "works." No one outside of us knows the inside of us better than we do. You can create a home environment that delights your spirit and surpasses your expectations.

I often find that, out of their vision and creativity, my clients end up designing beautiful environments that inspire me. Because these designs come out of them, they reflect who they are, their essential natures, their spirits. Their unique charm and beauty are projected into their environment. Having created something that exceeded their expectations, they are often surprised and delighted by the process and the result, something beautiful they hadn't known they were capable of creating.

There's no one true theory that will tell you how to transform your living environment into an altared space, or even how to turn your house into a beautiful home. But your consciousness, intentions, creativity and projections are an essential part of the process of creating a sacred environment in your home or office, and living a sacred life.

You may need a little help and guidance along the way. But the vision must come from or, at the very least, resonate profoundly within you. Only you are going to live in your space, not a professional designer or a feng shui master, not your friends and neighbors, not the photographer from *Better Homes and Gardens* or the film crew from *Lifestyles of the Rich and Famous.*

When you create a space that truly reflects and expresses who you are, the chances are that others, especially those who care about and matter to you, will love what you've done. They will feel welcome, connected, at ease and at home in your home, not because it's flawlessly designed or fabulously furnished but because it genuinely embodies and communicates something essential about you.

The best home design is always imperfectly perfect—not perfect for everyone, just perfect for us. It affirms and reflects who we are, our essential nature and who we desire to become in time. It nourishes, restores, inspires and uplifts the body, mind and spirit. And in doing all this, it fulfills the age-old promise of home as a healing sanctuary, as a reliable shelter from the storms of living in an uncertain world.

I intend for this book to show ordinary and remarkable people like you how to design your own altared space. My wish is that it support, inspire, assure and guide you as you contemplate and create the designs for your own altared space. May it lead you on a journey; open your eyes in new ways; and support, educate and inspire you to create the home of your dreams, right where you are, in your present circumstances, with the resources that you have. I know this is possible. May it be so for you.

SECTION ONE
WHAT IS SACRED?

WHAT IS SACRED?

W HETHER OR NOT WE CONSIDER OURSELVES SPIRITUAL OR RELIGIOUS, we all innately crave contact with something greater that restores and connects us to life. We long to feel happy, peaceful, comfortable in our own skin. We crave the feeling of completeness, of totality. We ache to feel that little chill that travels along the spine, tingles the skin and stirs the soul. Perhaps we pray for ourselves and for others to feel better, calmer and happier; or to be protected, loved and sustained. Basically we're all looking for a little more peace and security on earth, and a little more meaning and joy in life. These longings move us to reach toward that indefinable thing we call the sacred.

Many of us imagine we can only experience the sacred in formal settings, in designated places outside our homes that we have to dress up to visit, that we have to drive to in our cars and where we can only stay for a little while. So we may go to a church, temple, mosque, holy site or spiritual retreat. We may experience the sacred in nature. There are many ways to reconnect with the sacred.

Most of us have experienced the sacred in formal settings designed precisely for this purpose. There is often a mysterious—at times palpable—Presence that emanates from a sacred place. Not everyone knows it's possible to create our own sacred environments that invite and evoke this very Presence, and stir these feelings in us. Not everyone knows we can have this experience in our own homes every day; we can live naturally in an altared space.

Designing your home as a temple for your spirit doesn't mean you have to use overtly religious or spiritual imagery, but many people choose to do so. Let's consider some of the reasons behind this choice.

Churches, temples and other holy sites traditionally invoke the divine Presence and its spiritual protection. They do this through the use of sacred imagery, consciously arranged with spiritual intention and activated through ritual. The front of a sacred site is designed to make a powerful first impression, to shift us out of our mundane worldly consciousness, put us on our best behavior and prepare us to enter in an appropriate spirit. This serves those who enter the temple as well as the temple itself.

All aspects of a holy site are designed to enhance and deepen this initial effect. Sacred art—icons and statues, stained glass windows portraying spiritual figures and historical events, fountains and gardens, impressive architecture—all are designed to calm the mind, awaken the spirit, inspire reverence and induce contemplation. They remind us of God, the divine and the holiness of our own spirit. They invoke spiritual Presence and protection.

A friend recently told me the following story, which demonstrates the power of sacred imagery and spiritual intention to provoke a decisive response in others. A man he knew, who lived in New York City, was walking home from a late movie one Saturday night and took a shortcut through an unfamiliar neighborhood. As he turned a corner, just ahead he saw a group of tough-looking young men hanging out on the sidewalk, smoking cigarettes and talking. Their attention immediately turned to him and their conversation

stopped. At once the man knew that he was in their territory and was probably in trouble.

As he approached them, his adrenaline pumping with fear, they spread out across the sidewalk to block his path. Feeling helpless, he instinctively pressed his hands together in front of him and began whispering a desperate prayer, "Please God, help me get out of this…" As he drew near the young men, in his mind's eye he suddenly saw an image of himself walking toward them. He wore a nice black-leather jacket, zipped up to just below the collar, over a white turtleneck sweater. With his hands clasped in the prayer position, he realized that he resembled a priest. He experienced a surge of energy and the certainty that his prayer had been answered. He had been shown the way out. As he reached the young men, he raised his right hand in a gesture of blessing and said sincerely, "Bless you, my sons!"

Instantly, the atmosphere changed from one of menace to surprise and confusion. "Oh! Father!" one young man blurted apologetically.

They all stepped back, out of his way, opening a space to let the "priest" pass.

"Good evening, Father," said one, and then another, as he walked through.

"Bless you," said the man once more, and he meant it. He made it home safely.

These young men probably didn't consider themselves spiritual or religious, and their initial intentions were certainly less than benign. Yet they instinctively responded to the gesture of a ritual blessing from a man who appeared to be a priest, a sacred figure. And it called out the highest in them, just as they were about to act out their lower natures.

As you will see, you can use this principle to design your living space.

DESIGNING YOUR HOME CREATES TRUE OWNERSHIP

WHETHER YOU OWN OR RENT, YOUR HOME IS YOUR LIVING SPACE. But it only belongs to you spiritually to the degree that you invest yourself in it. Whether they are homeowners or not, many people live in their homes with a renter's mentality, with a feeling of temporariness that prevents them from fully investing their spirit into their environment. They may think they will begin when they have more money, more time, more opportunity, when their life is more together. If they "only rent," that becomes an excuse, and they imagine they will make a "real home" in the future when they own their home.

For any number of reasons, they never take the time to deeply examine and become conscious of the different spaces and energies in their home because they are waiting for something else to happen. Think about those friends of yours who say, "When I have X dollars, I will pursue my dream, start to give back, become a Big Brother, help build houses for Habitat for Humanity," and so on. If they ever do get more money, most never do those things because they've developed a habit of not investing themselves and of postponing their goals into a future that never quite arrives.

In the same way, many people never interact creatively with their home, never project their spirit and imagination into it, never turn it into the sacred space it could be. In some essential way, they never make their home, and perhaps even their life, their own.

Designing your living environment is the secret of ownership. Interior design is a way of projecting yourself, your vision, your spirit, your own unique "interior" into your home. It is a way to develop a conscious, creative, playful relationship with your living space. By investing your time, energy, imagination and money in your home, you

plant yourself in it, physically and spiritually. You don't just live in it; you completely inhabit it, own it and bring it to life. Your home becomes a living extension of who you are. It becomes a temple of your spirit, a place of renewal and restoration, a sanctuary for your life.

Conventional home design tends to view space as empty and needing to be filled, or as a blank canvas on which to impose such theoretical ideals as beauty, functionality, comfort, elegance and style. This approach can produce unique, elegant, beautiful and functional home designs that may please their owners, impress visitors and guests, and even make it into magazine photo shoots. But can someone else's theories and personal tastes create the perfect temple for *your* spirit, in *your* home?

When making such key decisions or changes as transforming our living environments, it is natural to experience moments of doubt: "Can I do this?" "Am I capable?" "Do I have good enough taste?" "Will my family and friends like it?" "Will they think I'm tacky, gaudy or gauche?" Such fears and doubts are common at various stages. They are the reason many people call in an expert designer. This book will help you navigate through your doubts. It will help you find clarity and confidence in your emerging personal vision. It will help you trust your gut, your unique tastes, your likes and dislikes, and all the choices you make along the way.

Suggestions and feedback can be helpful in the process, but no one else should become a higher authority or have final approval over the way you design your home. From beginning to end, your gut is your most reliable counsel, and each choice must be yours.

You'll know it's right when you feel that quality known in India as *sahej*, a yogic term loosely translated as that "Ahhhhh…" feeling in the gut when something hits the sweet spot. Your gut never lies. It should always have the final say. And if you follow this inner guidance, your new home environment will connect you to yourself and your vision. It will be your sacred space.

EVERYTHING IN OUR
ENVIRONMENTS AFFECTS US

AVE YOU EVER FELT IRRITABLE, annoyed or perhaps argumentative with your spouse for no apparent reason when you were out shopping? Have you felt rushed, distracted or spacey after spending a few minutes in a retail store? Have you ever walked into a restaurant, felt a little uncomfortable and walked out again moments later; or maybe you stayed and had a nagging feeling that you should have left? Perhaps the music was too loud or poorly chosen, the lighting too harsh or dim; maybe the tables felt cluttered or chaotic, the ambiance sterile or grungy, or something somehow just didn't feel right. Have you ever walked into the home of a friend or relative and immediately felt uncomfortable or ill at ease, perhaps for similar reasons?

These experiences are often the result of being in an unconscious environment. A conscious environment is designed to soothe the soul, relax the nervous system and make us feel at home. Even subtle things like lighting, color choices, smells and music can either soothe or disturb our senses, our consciousness and our subconscious.

Wherever we go, we are affected by our surroundings. We generally have little control over environments out in the world. Our homes are the most significant environments that we can control. We get to decide what we bring into or remove from our homes. We get to say what stays and what goes. We get to choose where we put things and how we arrange them. We can design our homes as we wish, according to our own visions. After being in the out-of-control world, we generally look forward to going home to be in the one place where we can relax, let go, feel safe and be completely ourselves.

So, when designing our living spaces, it is important to remember that everything we bring into our homes—each piece of furniture or art, every object, from a cushion to a copper saucepan—has its own feeling and creates an effect. Each combination of objects and elements—shapes, patterns,

colors, textures and scents—does the same. Every choice we make, practical or creative, also embodies a feeling and produces an effect. And the combination of all the elements together creates an environment, an ambiance, in the same way that all of the separate ingredients combined in a soup create the final flavor of the broth. So we need to be especially conscious about the things we bring into our homes. We need to consider, observe and consciously feel their effects on us. It's up to us to decide the effect we want our environments to have on us, and then consciously create environments that have that effect.

Ask yourself the following questions: "What do I want to see, feel and be surrounded by in my home? What do I want my living environment to look like and evoke in me? How do I want it to serve me?"

Everyone's tastes and desires differ. It's your tastes and desires that matter. Do you desire more beauty and style, more tranquility and harmony? Do you prefer Zen-like elegance, spare and understated, or plush comfort and

> *Wherever there is a touch of color,*
> *a note of a song, grace in a form,*
> *this is our call to love.*
> —RABINDRANATH TAGORE, NOBEL LAUREATE AND INDIAN POET, 1861–1941

a lavish look? Discover your own aesthetic. Trust yourself and your vision. This is essential to creating a unique, personal, meaningful environment where you will be happy living and sharing with your family and friends.

Sacred home design requires conscious reflection, a spiritual intention, some imagination and maybe a little education. In the process of designing your home, you'll develop a keener eye and a more refined sensibility. You'll become more attuned to the visual, sensual and spatial dimensions of your home. You'll also deepen your connection with yourself.

To create a home that is a temple for your spirit, you must know or discover what you really want, need, appreciate, desire and love. Then, by design, you can creatively anchor and evoke into your home any quality you choose and any feeling, meaning, mood or memory that you want present and alive in your life.

REENVISIONING ANY SPACE

A QUALITY LIVING DESIGN ISN'T CREATED IN A VACUUM or out of a theory. The person living in the space is essential to create a living environment that works for that individual at every level. The best home design is a creative projection into the environment of the person who lives there. And that person is you. So who you are, what you like and what makes you feel alive are essential to the process. When you project your vision, aesthetically and functionally, into three-dimensional space, you create a comfortable, delightful, beautiful environment that expresses and nurtures your essential self.

Our grace is making the invisible visible...
and the feelings of the heart when they
manifest are beauty itself. When others
see it, they attune to their own beauty.
So your designs are designs
for ecstatic, graceful living.

—DR. GURCHARAN KHALSA

To design a home that truly reflects and embraces you, that *you* find beautiful, pleasing and comfortable, it helps to view the space as if for the first time, with new eyes and a "beginner's mind." How can you see, from a new perspective, something you've grown used to, that you're utterly familiar with, that you take for granted?

To see your home with new eyes, you'll need to interact with it in a different way, look at it from different viewpoints. Most of us were taught to see space as empty or flat, or we were never taught to notice it at all. We notice objects and perimeters, but tend to ignore space and forget to take it into account. But space isn't empty or nonexistent. Every space has its own quality, depth and temperament.

When I help clients design their home interiors, I look through the rooms and spaces from multiple perspectives, from different physical locations. I also talk with them and get to know them a bit. I need to know some essentials about them to help them find their design. What are the essentials about you that you need to take into account in creating your own interior design?

For example, who else lives in your home with you? What are your practical needs? What experiences and activities do you want to have in any particular space? What are your emotional and spiritual needs? What feelings, reflections or memories do you want the space to evoke in you or invite you into? What part of yourself or your life do you want your home, or any space within it, to express? How do you want others to feel when they come to visit? Do you want your living environment to foster tranquility, harmony, playfulness, sensuality, creativity, inspiration or spirituality? What colors do you like? What kinds of images or art deeply affect you? What do you do for a living? What are your personal interests, your fascinations, your tastes in music, art, travel and life?

Walk through your home. Spend time in each room and each space you want to transform. Explore, pay attention and be present. Look, listen, feel and imagine into and through each space. Listen to the space. Listen to your gut. Listen to yourself the way you would listen to a child. Believe that your heart, creativity, consciousness, sacred intentions and positive projections combined can create a space that is loving, restorative and uplifting to you, your family and those who come to visit.

At different times of day, sit or stand in various areas in each room to get different perspectives. Investigate your home with a beginner's mind. Pretend you've never been there before, that you're seeing it for the first time. Listen to it, notice it, smell it, feel it. What do you see? What do you see past? What do you see through? How does it feel? How do the qualities of the space affect you? Are they calm, still, shadowy, flowing or bright? Do you feel comfortable? Are you restless? Are you centered and calm? What draws your eye from any point in the room?

What are the components in each room? Notice and feel the walls, their shadows as well as their colors. Are the colors stark, oppressive, bland? Are they warm, vibrant, soothing? Notice and feel the lighting. Do you like the fixtures? Turn the lights on and off. Are they too bright or too dim? How do they feel? What are

the particular needs of each room? Bathroom lighting ought to be bright, for good mirror reflection. We need to see ourselves clearly to shave, brush our hair, put on makeup, get ready for work or to go out on the town. Bedroom light should be softer, warmer, less intrusive.

What about the windows? Do you have quality curtains, basic white or off-white blinds? Do they feel good, or are they merely baseline functional? What would look and feel good with the furniture, lighting, carpets, paint, blinds? What do you really want? What would you love? What can you afford? What are your options? What is possible? What comes to mind as you look at any space and any component in any room? Ask yourself, how can this space be used? What could it look like? What would I like it to be? Ask yourself, how can this space serve me? Think creatively.

Do a slow walk-through of your home, starting outside the front entrance. What do you see when you approach the front door; when you first enter the house; as you walk, from different directions, through the house, down its halls, into and through its rooms? At each point, what naturally draws your attention?

As you do these exploratory exercises, keep a pen and notepad handy. Notice what opens up in you or becomes clear to you. Write down meaningful impressions and creative ideas that come to you. As you do these exercises, you'll feel your perspective shift as you access a new clarity and vision. This will help you make practical and creative choices that delight and feel right to you.

At some point you may feel intuitively drawn to certain colors, tones, images or other elements. You'll be intuitively guided to helpful information and resources. You'll want to do outside research: go to furniture stores, bookstores, the library; look at photographs in magazines, on websites and in books like this one.

You don't have to be an expert in sacred design to turn your home into an altared space. All it takes is some conscious reflection, some inspiration and maybe a little help. Then, in the process of doing it, you'll discover how to do it. The ideas, suggestions, exercises and photographs in this book will support you in this endeavor.

TAKING YOUR TIME
AND TRUSTING THE PROCESS

REMEMBER, YOUR COMMITMENT, INTENTIONS, vision and faith are the keys to creating a home that feels like home in every area, that is truly a temple for your spirit. So it's important not to pressure yourself or allow others to pressure you. Take your time, and let the process take its time. Don't rush things. Don't set arbitrary deadlines. Don't invite anyone into the process who will pressure you to rush decisions or criticize your choices, or whose motives or judgment you don't completely trust. Be aware that the emotional and energetic qualities you bring to this process will infuse and linger in your home.

A good therapist knows that when partners view one another as problems to be fixed, the relationship tends to degenerate into a battle of wills in which both partners lose, even when one apparently wins. A similar principle applies to home design. So don't approach your home negatively, as a problem to be fixed, but positively, as a creative challenge or opportunity. Approach it in a spirit of cooperation and enthusiasm. Be a partner with your home in the design process. Listen to your home, feel it, appreciate it. Cocreate with the way the energy of your home naturally flows. Follow its leanings. Adapt to its qualities. Let trust and enthusiasm inform the entire process from beginning to end.

Approaching your home design in this relational way is part of what will make it your temple. No object, statue or piece of furniture, no "correct" spiritual arrangement of elements, makes an environment sacred. Your visioning, intentions and involved relationship with each phase of the process are an investment of your spirit that makes your home sacred.

NO COMPANY CHEESE!

IN THE SAME WAY THAT OUR ATTITUDES and intentions can invoke the sacred, they can also banish the sacred by provoking tension, restlessness and discomfort. Our attitudes and priorities around the things in our homes, relative to the people who live there or come to visit, affect those people and our home environments.

Last year I went to a shop in Beverly Hills to buy some quality cheese. It was a reminder gift to my wife of our beautiful trip to Paris the previous Christmas. Many of the terrific meals we had eaten in the Parisian restaurants had involved delicious cheese. I bought a large wedge of very fine white truffle cheese, took it home and put it in the fridge. The next day I took it out, intending to sample it.

"Hey Jagatjoti," my wife said. "Should we save the cheese for company tonight?"

"Oh, this is *company* cheese?" I joked. "So we only get *house* cheese? I want *company* cheese!"

"I want company cheese, too!" said my almost three-year-old daughter. But she was completely serious. Soon she and I were chanting together, "We want company cheese! We want company cheese!"

Of course my wife appreciated my silly humor, and we all ended up eating company cheese. Company cheese is now a family joke. But it points to a real principle about how to live, and not live, in our own homes. The principle is this: first and foremost, home should serve the people who live there. But sometimes we set up a home environment for the benefit of others, at the expense of those who live in it. This is a company-cheese mentality. It creates

*Did you ever see an unhappy horse? Did you ever see a bird that had the blues? One reason why birds and horses are not unhappy is because they are **not trying to impress** other birds and horses.*

— DALE CARNEGIE

tension and discomfort, and makes people (usually the children) second-class citizens in their own homes.

That was the problem in the perfect designer home in which I grew up. For example, our dining room had a beautiful mahogany table. God forbid that it should've ever been scratched or eaten at, for that matter. Heaven help us if it ever suffered a water stain! So I never felt comfortable at that table. It was a company table in a company room. I only sat there once or twice a year for family holidays. The rest of the time we ate at the table in the kitchen.

So I don't believe in having "company" furniture, food, rooms or spaces in a home. Nothing kills an altared space like the feeling that you don't belong or aren't welcome. A home feels best when everyone who lives there feels welcome and at home in every part (although we ought to have privacy and dominion in our own bedrooms). No company cheese!

In this spirit, I suggest not buying furniture that, if it got scratched or stained in the course of living, would ruin your day. Do not buy furniture that, if your child opened it or hid something in it, would make you feel that you'd been violated. Don't buy "freak-out" furniture that, if someone went near it or used it without following specified protocols, would send you into semi–rigor mortis. Don't invest furniture and other home items with your neuroses. No company furniture! Let it all be used!

When things in a home become more important than the peace and comfort of the people who live there, you no longer have an altared space. If you have a fine wooden table that you don't want to get water–stained, keep plenty of coasters available or be willing to refinish it later with no regrets or complaints. Better yet, don't worry on principle.

Furniture that you worry about becomes a potential booby trap in your home. Such pieces become magnets, attracting the very things that will blow up your peace of mind and drive you crazy. They will create subliminal tension in you, your family, your guests and your home. As a child, did you ever go to the home of a friend to find plastic covers on their living room couches and chairs? If you're like me, it didn't make you feel welcome or at home. Our use and enjoyment of the things in our homes ought to be a higher priority than whether or not they get scratched, nicked, marked or stained over time.

A company-cheese mentality is a kind of stinginess or poverty consciousness. It's about controlling, hoarding or holding tightly onto things. It's similar to a miser living in poverty with a fortune hidden under the mattress. Be expansive in your home! Let it all be available for use! Let the living commence! Let everyone eat the company cheese!

DESIGN AS RITUAL

THERE ARE MANY REASONS FOR DESIGNING or redesigning our homes. Each home-design project usually involves a variety of reasons. Our reasons may be very practical. We may simply want to make our living environments more functional, comfortable, beautiful, elegant or modern. We may want an upgrade, with better-quality furniture, carpet, tile, lighting, cabinets, and interior and exterior paint. One may have an abundance of funds and decide that home is a good place to invest it. Perhaps we're in transition and see an opportunity to make practical and creative changes and improvements in our environments. Maybe we've bought a new home; we're relocating; we've gotten married, divorced or widowed; we're downsizing or upgrading; we're moving up in the world or even across the world.

Yet there are often deeper reasons motivating one to create a new home environment. If our houses truly do represent our deepest selves, then consciously or not, redesigning our homes is a powerful way of reconceiving, redefining and expressing who we are, or who we are becoming. Transforming our homes can be part of a process of reinventing ourselves; a way of marking or ritualizing significant personal changes, phases and transitions in our lives; or a beautiful and creative way to support and facilitate life transitions and to anchor desirable new elements in our living environments. We can get as much inner mileage out of redesigning our homes as we choose. We are only limited by our imaginations.

For example, one of my clients, a single woman who hadn't been in a relationship in years, felt a strong desire to change her life on many levels. She owned a beautiful home that was elegantly and

tastefully designed. But now she felt that her home, with all its familiar associations, represented her old self, the self she was in the process of changing. Her home environment somehow seemed to keep her in the orbit of her old life.

Since she loved her home, selling it seemed too drastic. So she decided to create an entirely new home environment, one that would support the changes she wanted to make, reflect her newly emerging sensibilities and desires, fully nurture the new person she was becoming, and invite love and intimacy into her home and life. That was the vision and intention she created for herself through her home-design project—and that was the result she got.

I've worked with client couples who decided to redesign their homes together as a way to reconnect with each other and rekindle their relationships. I've worked with writers and artists who redesigned their homes, or specific rooms within their homes, to nurture and stimulate creativity. I've helped couples design tantric bedrooms as sensual playrooms to spice up their marriages and love lives. I've helped people design dining rooms that would inspire people to come to the table and linger longer after the meal was done. You can design your home or any part of it for any purpose you can conceive. And, if consciously executed, your purpose will bear fruit. I've seen it happen time and again.

Designing your home is a practical, creative and spiritual process. As you redesign and transform your external living environment in a way that pleases, delights and inspires you, you reprogram your own psyche and your environment, for new and positive life experiences. And the process of rediscovering, reconceiving and transforming your living environment produces corresponding changes in you. Something new awakens inside of you.

Make a list of all the reasons that might underlie your desire to redesign your home. Are you experiencing changes, growth or upheaval? Do you want to create an environment that will support or invoke more creativity, love, peace, joy or stability in your life? Are you looking for spiritual renewal, a way to initiate growth and change on deeper levels? Do you want your home to more accurately reflect and embody who you are now, or who you're becoming? What would you like to get out of the process besides the end result of a beautifully designed home? Think outside the box! Don't set limits on the experience or the end result!

SECTION TWO

THE ALTAR

THE ALTAR

ALTARS OF VARIOUS KINDS PLACED THROUGHOUT your home can be an effective and beautiful motif, one that helps to create a conscious, serene and temple-like environment.

For many centuries and in many cultures, the altar has been the spiritual heart of both temple and home. Historically, for families and communities, the altar has played an integral role in defining, invoking and keeping alive the experience of the sacred.

Traditional altars are a ritual arrangement of sacred objects. In this sense they are a kind of miniature stage, and the ceremonies performed there are a kind of sacred theater designed to sanctify and bless, to invoke the attention and presence of the Divine and to usher participants into states of spiritual awareness. Traditional altar objects may include incense, candles, fire, water, oil, ash, statues, icons, spiritual books, natural elements and even the bones and ashes of saints or cherished spiritual figures.

Altars have always been places for formal transactions between the human and divine realms. Altars are where spiritual renunciates, pilgrims, devotees and laymen come to worship, meditate and pray; offer gifts; and perform acts of devotion. The altar is where the individual soul lays down and offers up its troubles, problems, fears and concerns, and surrenders to its Creator. In return, the soul receives divine blessings and is relieved of spiritual burdens.

The traditional offerings of flowers, money, fruits, sweets and gifts, laid on the altar before worship, represent the Self and all its attachments surrendered to God. And the fruits and sweets traditionally distributed from the altar after worship represent the blessings of the Divine, and also the surrendered Self returned, purified and sanctified by the Divine. For all of the above reasons, the altar embodies the fundamental principles and ideals of sacred design.

The traditional Western family altar is often personal and archetypal in its array of objects, evoking and honoring our personal histories and our blood lineages, and giving context to our place in the present by acknowledging our ancestral roots. A common Western altar resides on the mantle above the fireplace, with its array of family photos, letters, personal mementos, knickknacks and handed-down family treasures often going back for generations.

But an altar doesn't have to follow a specific format. It can be whatever we make it or need it to be. And it can evolve and change as we do. Because the sacred responds to our intentions and faith, we can make an altar of any size or design, in any location, for any purpose or need. Because altars are extensions of ourselves and our souls, they can reflect our ideals, passions, interests, goals and dreams, and can be composed of any objects, elements, sounds, scents and imagery that are meaningful to us.

Any place that we declare, design and serve as sacred becomes an altar. A bedroom dresser top, a bathroom or kitchen countertop, a living room coffee table, a built-in nook in a hallway or stairway, or a closet—all are suitable locations for a household altar. It can be the dramatic focal point of a formal prayer and meditation space. It can be a small fountain surrounded by flowers in a garden corner. It can even be, and often is, a refrigerator door.

There are many altars in my home. The small altar in my front entryway reminds me that my life is full of God, guru and family. It has a water bowl with floating flowers, a picture of Guru Nanak and a picture of my family. There is an altar on the dresser in the bedroom where my wife and daughter put statues, pictures and gathered treasures from our journeys together. We have a living room altar where we put holiday cards from our friends and family, checks received from clients, bills to pay, special objects we've bought, gifts we've received, gifts we're going to give to others, and pictures of friends and family we want to hold in a sacred light. This is how we acknowledge our relationships and business as sacred occupations, and offer them to God. It is a place where we let go and let God take care of it all.

Because the sacred responds to our intentions and faith, we can make an altar of any size or design, in any location, for any purpose or need.

AN ANTIQUE ALTAR (left)
The couple that owns this house was planning their wedding and wanted an altar to bless the event, to greet family and friends at the reception and as a place to leave gifts and cards. Both were raised devout Catholics, and their faith is central to their lives. This altar now graces their living room.

Common things people place on home altars

- Fruit, fresh herbs or flowers picked each day from your garden.
- Spiritual icons, statues and framed pictures connected to your particular path or faith.
- Sacred items such as holy ash, oil or incense from ashrams, temples and churches.
- Personal items with special meaning or emotional value, for example, photographs, paintings, drawings, found objects or mementos acquired during travels.
- Sensual items such as incense and essential-oil–infused candles (for example, mint for awakening or lavender for calming).
- A wish box or God box. This can be a wooden box, a ceramic container, or even a leather or silk pouch. A wish box or God box is a place to put pieces of paper on which we've written our wishes, hopes and dreams; our problems and concerns; or our prayers for others and even their photos. By placing them in the box with a prayer or meditation, we symbolically surrender them into God's hands. Reviewing these notes later, you will often find that problems have been resolved, wishes have been fulfilled and goals have been (or are becoming) achieved; and individuals prayed for have in fact been helped or healed.
- Beads and jewelry such as malas, rosaries, crystals or more personal jewelry items.
- Advertisements, pictures and images of things you want to work toward, whether material, emotional, spiritual or physical. These images can involve anything that symbolizes your particular activity, goal or dream.
- Pictures of a friend or family member whom you want to pray for because they are physically or mentally ill.
- Anything else that you feel moved to place on your altar.

FINDING AND PLACING FURNITURE, ART AND OBJECTS

IN CHOOSING DESIGN OPTIONS it's important to know each room's purpose for you and your family. How do you want the room to feel? What activities will occur there? What qualities and consciousness do you want to anchor, enhance and experience there—calmness, patience, comfort, vitality, prosperity, sacredness? Whatever qualities you choose, you can create an environment that reflects and serves them.

Now the task is to creatively discover how that would look to *you*. Be sure to examine and choose every item with your eye and your gut. Every item should be a meaningful anchor for something—a memory, mood or feeling. If it has no meaning for you, if it doesn't palpably stir, please or nourish you, it probably doesn't belong in your home.

Think of each object in your home as a musical note or chord, the empty spaces as the silences between the notes, and the creative combination of all of the objects and spaces in your home as a melody or symphony. Your challenge is to discover, perhaps note by note and space by space, the melody of your home design. To do that, you need to tune into and feel each item, each piece of art and furniture, and the space itself. Then, make sure each note resonates in your gut. That's how you know it's the right note.

Mark Twain said, "The difference between the right word and almost the right word is the difference between lightning and a lightning bug." It's the same when it comes to choosing, purchasing and placing items for your home. In choosing furnishings and art, each piece and its placement should feel exactly right, as if hitting the bull's-eye in your gut, or playing the right note in a beautiful melody. Look for the false notes, the ones that appear right but don't resonate with your depths. Comfort and aesthetics are important, but that lightning factor is what makes a note the perfect note. Why bring anything less into your altared space?

Even when your eye and mind are confused, your gut still knows the difference between lightning and a lightning bug. So take your time with each piece, feel how it makes you feel and don't settle for almost. Remember, home design is not about filling empty space with stuff, even impressive stuff. It's about creating the most comfortable and beautiful environment that speaks to your spirit and sensibilities, and meets your particular needs. It isn't about impressing others. It's about you loving what you buy and put in your home. It's about you loving how it all fits together and how you feel in it.

In terms of furniture placement, don't crowd yourself by putting things too close together. A room shouldn't be a maze or an obstacle course you have to negotiate daily. You want relatively easy access when passing through any room or moving from one part of a room to another.

Also, a limited budget doesn't have to limit your satisfaction with the final result. The perfect pieces for you, or for any space in your home, aren't necessarily the most expensive, stylish or original, or the ones the salesperson says are top of the line. They're the pieces that ring your bell. And you can find them in unexpected places and in many home furniture outlets.

If you find something you love but can't afford, don't worry. Be patient and keep looking. You will be able to find something affordable that you also love, and that perfectly fits your home, needs and tastes. Or, you can wait and save up for something you love but can't afford right now. It's your choice. Just don't settle for lightning bugs. Hold out for lightning and it will come as unexpectedly as lightning often does.

The right timing may not necessarily conform to your initial schedule. Be willing to let the process take the time it needs to come together. Selecting and buying things in a rush to meet a hasty home-design deadline is almost never a good idea. Let it be an unfolding creative quest. Go on a pilgrimage to stores in your area. Search the Web. Read home-design magazines. Look until you find things that you know, with absolute confidence, will work for you and your home.

We all need a little help and support when making important decisions. Good feedback, genuine expertise and a different perspective are useful. So get good help if you can find it. Invite a friend or acquaintance into the process, one who knows you and whose taste you trust. Seeing things through someone else's eyes can expand and clarify your own vision. You can also use a professional designer or shopper, someone who has greater knowledge in this area, knows where to find things, and brings a broader and more seasoned perspective to the process.

But, bottom line, only buy stuff you *really* like and that you think you'll still like when your income grows, you move, or you remodel your house. Trust that you can, right where you are, with your present budget, design a beautiful home environment where you feel completely comfortable, at ease and connected to all that surrounds you in any room you enter.

TEXTILES AND ACCESSORIES: TEXTURE MAKES ALL THE DIFFERENCE

ALL HUMANS RESPOND TO TOUCH, as is reflected in textile grades and values. We have silk, satin, fur, velvet, wool, cashmere and cotton. We have brushed, waffled, ribbed, rough or raw.

Personally, I think we ought to pay as much attention to what we wrap around our bodies as to what we put into them. Most of us unwittingly wrap or cover ourselves in materials that have been heavily treated with toxic pesticides. Traditionally cotton sheets are the norm for bedding. They are more body-friendly, more comfortable and of better quality than synthetic fabrics. But shockingly, in the United States, one fourth of all pesticides used are applied to one crop—cotton. According to www.sustainablecotton.org, roughly a third of a pound of synthetic fertilizers and pesticides are used to grow enough cotton for a T-shirt. And cotton grown in third-world countries isn't much better. Scary, isn't it?

I recommend supporting healthy, eco-friendly businesses and reducing the health risks for your family by purchasing organic cotton sheets and clothing. A number of organic-cotton sheet sets with thread counts of over six hundred are available for under a hundred dollars. Thousand—thread-count organic sets are available for the luxury shopper. For the sake of my family, I want every item and bit of energy in the bedroom, and especially on the bed, to be energetically and chemically positive, peaceful, healthy and pure.

Cheap carpeting and bed accessory fabrics are harsh on the body. They disturb the subconscious and create disharmony, making you feel less than completely relaxed. Part of this effect is the quality of the item itself. Another part is the message you give yourself when you buy inferior bedroom items. You're basically telling yourself, "You're not worth the extra expense." Since our bedrooms are where we spend most of the time in our homes, and where we seek maximum rest and restoration, I recommend investing in quality when it comes to bedroom carpets, blankets, sheets, pillows and pillowcases. You don't have to buy absolutely top of the line, but buy quality. In this arena in particular, the difference between cheap items and quality items is noticeable.

LIGHTING

LIGHTING CAN MAKE OR BREAK THE ATMOSPHERE in a room. It can highlight or hide items and direct, divert or assault the eye. Proper lighting is essential to create an environment of relaxation, comfort and functionality in any room. Effective use of lighting sets the stage. The ideal lighting generally casts a warm glow, enveloping everything in a soft golden light. Dimmer switches that allow a range from soft to bright are always good. Side lighting is practical and convenient. Putting small soft-light lamps on either side of the bed can create an intimate atmosphere perfect for nighttime chatting, bedtime reading or late-night trips to the bathroom. Family reading may call for additional task lighting, for which floor lamps are ideal. The key is having just enough light so that reading doesn't strain your eyes, but not so much light that your inner circadian rhythms are thrown off.

The human nervous system is extremely sensitive to light. Your body responds to the brightening or softening of the light around you whether you notice it or not. Gradually turning down your bedroom

lights with a dimmer switch as bedtime approaches signals your body that it is time to rest. Just before going to sleep, you may choose to turn off all your bedroom lights and rely solely on candlelight, the softest and most therapeutic light you can bring into a bedroom. Also, you may choose strategic placement of night-lights in different parts of the house, depending on your nighttime habits.

SCENT

L IKE LIGHTING, SCENT HAS A VISCERAL EFFECT ON US, at both conscious and subliminal levels. Familiar scents from childhood often trigger sudden experiential childhood memories. The right scent for us shifts our consciousness and moves us into more pleasurable and relaxed states. The wrong scent can do the opposite. When it comes to choosing scents for our environments, natural and organic are always best, since many scent products use unhealthy chemicals. Several excellent options for bedroom scents include fresh flowers, scented or essential oils, natural incense and scented candles. For safety, candles should always be placed away from linens and bed sheets, on a stable, nonflammable surface. It is important to investigate candle options, noting the different types of wax and wicks. Some candles give off quite a bit of smoke, which isn't a scent you want permeating your bedroom.

Smokeless candles are available. Large, stable candle bowls filled with soy wax and non-lead wicks are safe and ideal for bedroom use. If you choose incense, use your discretion, since smoke is the medium of the scent. My favorite incenses are Zhingkham Kunchhab Chhoetrinm, from Bhutan, and Tara, from India. Both are made from a mix of several-dozen healing and fragrant herbs and spices, and are commonly used by lamas and monks in Buddhist temples. I also like Rain, Arabian Musk and many kinds of Japanese incense, all of which are fairly commonly available.

MUSIC

B ECAUSE NOTHING CAN CHANGE, STIR, elevate, calm and engage us like the sacredness of sound, music is also a powerful element in creating a home temple. As with lighting and scent, our nervous systems are extremely responsive to music. Be sensitive to your own needs and your nervous system in your choice and timing of the music you play. Consciously choose music that creates the effect you want, depending on the room, the occasion, or the time of day or night.

In February 2005, the *Journal of Advanced Nursing* reported that older people with sleep problems noted a 35 percent improvement after they started listening to forty-five minutes of soft music before bedtime. After the disastrous hurricane season of 2005, FEMA recommended

creating and listening to music as a way to reduce tension and relieve extreme stress. Music also affects the quality of sleep in both adults and children.

Whether you like classical, jazz, rock, world beat, easy listening or traditional music of any culture or period, the music that stirs your soul is your sacred music. Personally, I find mantra music perfect for setting the tone for the house. You may want to vary the music depending on the occasion. What do you like to listen to when you're cooking in the kitchen? When you're reading or relaxing in the living room or bedroom? When you're winding down before bed, meditating, making love, waking up in the morning or preparing for your day?

Music is nice to go to bed to and to wake up to. For music lovers, I recommend a stereo with a sleep timer that turns your music off at night and on again in the morning.

Music is also a way to "altar" your space while traveling, which I do quite often. You can't control the lighting or light a stick of incense on an airplane, but you can carry with you meditation music, mantras and sacred sounds. That's what I do. And it makes me feel more at home on the road by changing my vibrations and the vibrations of the space I happen to be in, whether an airport, taxi or hotel room.

STORAGE: KEEPING IT NEAT

CLUTTER CAN ALL TOO EASILY CREEP INTO and take over any part of our living environments, distracting and detracting from the ultimate goal of relaxation and restoration. Clothes, books and other items scattered on the floor, the bed, chairs and tables increasingly add up to chaos. Clutter interferes with our physical environments, our visual fields and our minds by gnawing at the subconscious and physically getting in the way. Ignoring clutter isn't the solution, as this only desensitizes and distances us from the home environment that ought to open up and nourish us.

There are many easy, ingenious, affordable, hidden storage solutions for your home. These include a wide variety of closet organizers, mini-storage and shelving systems, and outdoor portable storage units. More elegant storage solutions may include quality cabinets, wardrobes, dressers, armoires, trunks and more. Whichever solution you choose, it's important to take storage into account when creating a conscious, orderly, uncluttered home.

There are two ways of living in
this world: the way of worry and
the way of relaxation.
If you worry, you have to
concentrate to imagine, and it becomes
physical work.
But if you turn your
mind to the Universal Mind,
then things will come to you.

— YOGI BHAJAN

COLORS: SETTING THE TONE

WE'VE KNOWN FOR AGES, since long before the advent of color therapy, that various colors express and stimulate diverse moods, reflections and responses. Colors can energize and stimulate, calm and refresh, and even inspire and heal us. Red famously draws attention and stimulates decidedly energetic, aggressive or erotic responses. Matadors wave red flags at bulls to provoke aggression. It's no coincidence that sexual zones around the world are called red-light districts. Statistically police pull over more red cars annually than cars of any other color. Blues and greens tend to relax, soothe and calm, which is why talk-show guests often wait in a "greenroom" before going out to face lights, cameras and audiences.

Because colors do affect us, it's important to choose carefully the color schemes in our living environments. Colors can soften or mute a room, tone it down. They can make a room warmer and cozier. They can energize a room, making us feel more awake, creative and alive. The key to choosing a color scheme for any room is knowing what we want to experience and how we want to feel in that room. Then we can explore the range of color options and pick the right colors for the right room.

The primary determining factor in any color choice is what *you* like, whether strong, flamboyant colors, rich primary colors, airy pastels or simple conservative shades. Experiment with one wall or area of a room. Be creative, even playful. Liberally paint your chosen color there or roll wide swaths, vertical or horizontal, of possible colors on different walls. Then let it dry. Sit with it for a while. Sleep on it. See how it looks in various shades of light at different times of day or night. Notice how it draws your eye, how it makes you feel.

Below is a brief general description of the basic effects of colors on the human psyche.

Pink	Physically, mentally and emotionally soothing. It enlivens compassion, love and purity.
Yellow	Awakening and mentally activating. It stimulates intellectual activity.
Red	Stimulates the mind and body. It encourages sexuality and passion. It can be extreme and very powerful. Use it wisely and sparingly.
Green	Brings balance, encourages growth and instills calm.
Blue	Enhances creative expression. It is peaceful and expansive, like the sky.
Purple	Has a hypnotic effect. It encourages intense emotions, from anger to sublimity. It should be used very sparingly.
Orange	Activates optimism and refuels energy reserves.

SECTION THREE
A WALK-THROUGH

THE FRONT EXTERIOR:
THE FACE OF HOME

I N PSYCHOLOGICAL TERMS, your home is a symbol and reflection of yourself. Given this, the front of your home represents the "face" you present to the outside world. It is the first and most prominent part of your home (and you) that everyone can see. In designing your home, it helps to view the front of it as a primary communication and expression of yourself to the outside world.

When President Lincoln was choosing the members of his cabinet, a close associate recommended a certain man. President Lincoln immediately dismissed the suggestion and, when asked the reason why, simply said, "I don't like his face."

"But the poor man isn't responsible for his face," responded Lincoln's associate.

Lincoln replied, "Every man over forty is responsible for his face."

In terms of home design, you are responsible for the face of your home and what it communicates to the outside world. Whether it is beautiful or shabby, imposing or humble, well tended or unkempt, strikingly original, or generic and nondescript, the front of your home is a kind of public billboard that, to some degree, communicates a message and makes an impression on all who pass by. And as more people pass by your home than enter it, the front of your home is the only encounter with you that many people ever have.

First impressions stir instinctive feelings and responses and set up subtle expectations in others. This is true with our homes. The front of your home is the place to decide what effect you want to have and what kind of impression you want to make on anyone who passes by or enters, including you. It's not about your ego or impressing others. It's about taking responsibility for the inevitable effect you have, and consciously choosing what that will be. It's about

using this first impression as an opportunity to contribute something of your essential self to the world.

How would you like others to feel when they're with you? How would you like them to feel about you? What do you want to offer or inspire in them? How do you want to greet them as they approach your domain?

Take a few moments to consider these questions: What does the front of your home reveal and express about you right now? What does it communicate and offer to others? Is it conscious? Is it harmonious? Is it chaotic? What impressions, feelings or reflections does it evoke or inspire? How does it greet and affect you and your family each time you come home? How does it greet and affect friends and relatives when they come to visit? Have you consciously designed it with a specific intention, as described above?

In our busy and often hectic modern lives, it's easy to choose, by default, a generic look for the front of our homes. A basic front lawn with maybe a tree and some shrubbery can be sufficient. There's nothing wrong with this. But with a little thought, imagination and conscious intention, it's possible to do much more.

The idea of the home as a temple is one reason many people choose to have sacred statuary, beautiful vases, plants and flowers, elegant wind chimes, fountains with running water and more in front of their homes. The following photographs show a conscious temple approach to the front of a home.

This is a simple house in a nice L.A. neighborhood, on a block of other very similar houses. The owners wanted this house to be what many of us want our homes to be—a temple, a place of calmness and restoration, a spiritually empowered and protected environment. They wanted the protection invoked in a sacred space, protection without armor and fear—no iron gates, security cameras or barred windows. They wanted their house to be a sanctuary from the world and also a blessing in the world.

So they picked two large stone Buddha statues that embodied the energy and intention they wanted to project and offer to the outside world. They made a conscious decision that the front of their home would be an expression and reminder of the sacred. These Buddha statues evoke the feelings and reflections the homeowners want to experience and be reminded of each time they approach and enter their home.

These stone Buddhas are the guardians of their gate and the spiritual benefactors of their sanctuary. They are sacred images offering spiritual blessing to all who approach or pass by, and spiritual protection to those who enter.

Remove these statues and this home becomes much like all the other homes on the block. This isn't necessarily a bad thing. But these owners wanted something more, something different, something that fulfilled their particular needs and reflected something deeper about them.

THE ENTRYWAY

YOUR FRONT ENTRYWAY IS THE THRESHOLD, the place of transition between the outside world and your inner sanctum. Ideally the first step into your house ought to lead you, visually and symbolically, across a threshold into a place of ever-deepening restoration.

In many households and cultures it is customary to remove one's shoes when entering through the front door. This is a way to literally leave the energy and dust of the world behind and to keep the home a sanctuary, set apart from the world.

Whether a front entrance opens into a narrow hallway with a utility closet, a courtyard or a grand foyer with marble tile and a winding staircase, it should set the mood for the home and arouse feelings in the people who live there. Regardless of the size or shape of your entryway, you can design it to create any mood or feeling you desire. Like the introduction to a book, this first step into your home sets a tone, an imprint. Whatever is there greets and impacts everyone who enters.

Front entryways all too easily succumb to clutter and disorganization. They are the place where shoes, coats, mail, keys, spare change and other miscellaneous objects tend to gather. Creating an entryway altar helps you keep your home conscious, orderly and serene. Consider it a kind of spiritual customs stop where you relinquish, hopefully for the duration of your stay, the chaos and unconsciousness, the concerns and distractions—the "contraband"—of your worldly life.

Your front entrance doesn't have to be fancy, formal, gaudy or over the top. Beauty and elegance are at home in humility and

simplicity. Ideally, a front entryway invokes calm, elegance and instills an immediate sense of ease. It reminds us of who we are and what we cherish most. It soothes the soul, calms the consciousness and reminds us of what the inner life is really about.

When I open the door to my home, the first thing I see in the entryway is an elegant stand that has a bowl full of water with a flower floating on top. The flower floating in the top of the bowl reminds me that no matter how apparently full to the brim my life is, there is always room for God. Behind the bowl, there are always one or two pictures of spiritual figures and my family, including my wife and child. There is a small statue and a scented candle. I occasionally change the objects

to vary the impressions and moods. Yet this harmoniously arranged entryway altar always greets me and prepares me to enter my home in a spirit of peace, gratitude and reverence. In what spirit do you want to enter your home? Knowing this will help you design your own entryway.

Do the following experiment. Go out of your house, and then come back in with fresh eyes. Notice what you see and how you feel as you open your front door and step inside. Where is your eye immediately drawn? What objects, lighting and aromas greet you? Is your entryway conscious, beautiful, meaningful, intentional? Is it cluttered, random and chaotic? Is it merely functional and utilitarian? Does it help you become conscious, to let go of your worldly concerns and enter your home in a right spirit?

As you enter your home, allow this first emotional impact of your entryway to wash over you, to sink in. Is this what you want your family, friends, guests and yourself to see and feel on entering?

Now imagine walking into a home consciously and lovingly designed by you, your spouse and perhaps even your children. What images, objects, scents and feelings greet you as you open your front door? Do they speak to your personal history, unique sensibilities, imagination and spirit? Do they invite you to leave behind the hustle, bustle and chaos of the world and enter into a serene, nourishing environment where you can relax, open up and let go?

Consider your entrance in the light of these ideas and these photographs.

THE DINING ROOM:
NOURISHMENT FOR BODY AND SOUL

FOR MANY, THE DINING ROOM IS THE HEARTH of the home, a place where the body is nourished and the soul fed. It is a place for family meals, holiday celebrations, coffee, conversations and breaking bread with old and new friends. It is a primary location in most homes where we connect in relationship through ritual sharing of food and social conviviality.

The first clue that a dining room isn't working is when it becomes a place, not to relax and savor, but to chew and bolt. This was the case for one of my clients. Her family tended to rush through dinner and leave the table immediately afterward. Even guests seemed less than comfortable at the dinner table and eager to retire to the living room when the meal was over. She asked me to come and look at the dining room to help her figure out why and what to do about it.

When I got there, I noticed several things. The dining room was open and spacious, but the lighting was bright to the point of harshness. The walls were empty and painted a stark white. As a result, the room had no warmth or personality; it was a sterile environment. That wasn't the only factor.

The dining-room table and chairs were of excellent quality. But the table and chairs had hard, sharp edges, and the table was a bit high relative to the chairs, which seemed to push you back and away, to separate you from guests on the other side of the table. All of these things combined to create a sense of distance and discomfort. Sitting at that table in that room was not relaxing or enjoyable.

There are usually very practical and solvable reasons why rooms don't work. Such rooms are often baseline environments that are not consciously designed to make us feel relaxed and comfortable. A well-designed room serves our practical needs and has warmth and feeling that resonate with us. It makes us feel at home. Other than that, there are no hard and fast design rules or rigid conventions that absolutely must be followed.

For instance, your dining room can be a formal, elegant

space or a casual hanging-out place. It doesn't have to have a traditional matching table with chairs as a central focus. The Japanese do fine with a low table and floor cushions. You'll notice a variation on this model in the photos that follow, with a large, low table that is also an altar, set unconventionally against a wall, with plush floor cushions for seating. The couple that owns this home throws large parties where everyone sits on cushions on the floor. The children especially love it!

These dining-room photographs range from elegant formal to kick-back casual. You can imagine feeling nourished by any of these following settings while enjoying a good meal, coffee or conversation.

The dining room is a primary location in most homes where we connect in relationship through ritual sharing of food and social conviviality.

THE LIVING ROOM:
THE RENAISSANCE OF THE FAMILY ROOM

IF THE DINING ROOM IS A PLACE FOR EATING; the living room is a place for being. It is perhaps the most public and multifunctional room in the house. Here we gather and socialize with family and friends, watch movies or TV, relax and nap on the couch, play games, read on rainy days or weekends, hang out with the children or simply sit in the atmosphere, doing nothing at all.

An ideal living room is a place that draws you and others, one where you feel nurtured and comfortable. Traditionally the living room is the central room in the home, but it doesn't have to be traditional. It doesn't have to be a showcase room. It can be as formal, casual, whimsical or exotic as you are, or as you want it to be. Again, the bottom line is that it delights your eye and sensibilities, serves your practical needs, has warmth and personality and makes *you* feel at home. It should be a space that allows all the moods of your life—the fun and lighthearted, the sensual and serene, the quirky and creative, the sublime and spiritual.

Many people like to go the formal route with their living rooms. Conservative leather couches and chairs, stately polished cabinets and tables, fine rugs or quality carpeting, traditional art, cherished family portraits and heirlooms and, of course, quality lighting can all add up to a stunning and elegant central room in your home temple.

Your living room can also be as original and eclectic as your personality and history. This is the living room as personal museum or visual biography, a three-dimensional mosaic of images, objects and treasures acquired in the course of your life adventures. You can have unconventional, offbeat couches, chairs, cabinets, lamps and tables;

lively colors, fabrics and patterns; unusual carpets, rugs or wall hangings; lots of plush pillows and even beanbag chairs.

My living room is designed for my family's particular needs, as well as for beauty and comfort. Because we have a young child, all the furniture is soft or has rounded edges. The arrangement of elements is orderly and spacious, and the pathways are clear. We have an altar with statues and figurines. My daughter, Pritam, is welcome to open, close, play with, touch and enjoy everything in the living room—and she knows it. *Everything* that's within her reach is fine for her to touch, pick up and play with. We have pledged not to make the living room mantra, "Don't touch that." After all, it is her home also. Anything we'd rather she not play with is well out of reach, on high shelves or inside cabinets. I designed the space for how we want to live in it, feel in it, be in it and move through it. It's perfect for where we are in our lives right now.

The main factor in creating an environment is that it be consistent within itself, and have its own singular harmony, mood and expression. As with all design, this singular harmony will come out of you, and you'll recognize when it's there. The only limits are your imagination and your patience with, and commitment to, the process. The X factor to look for is that spark of inspiration that emerges once you open to it and are willing to rely on it. And, as always, the final arbiter is your gut.

*A well-designed room serves our practical needs and has **warmth and feeling** that resonate with us.*

ALTARING YOUR BATHROOM:
SETTING THE MOOD OF THE DAY

OUR BATHROOMS ARE OFTEN THE FIRST and last places we spend significant functional time each day, an average of thirty minutes daily for most of us. Other than the kitchen, the bathroom is the most functional room in most homes, and it is by far the most visually oriented. Mirrors and lighting, water and plumbing, sink, toilet and tub all define the bathroom environment. A place of cleansing, elimination and detoxification, it's where we brush our teeth, wash our hands and face, care for our skin, shave, put on makeup, refine and double-check our appearance, and prepare to meet the outside world. It is also where we scrub and wash the last remnants of the world down the drain before going to sleep at night.

Our bathrooms ought to help us make the most out of these minutes. But more than just serving these functional purposes, the bathroom can also be a healing environment, delightful to the eye and the senses that begins and completes our restoration each day. Whether you design your bathroom from scratch by putting in new cabinets, lighting, hardware, wallpaper or paint, or you design it around the essential items and elements already in place, the suggestions below will help you enhance your bathroom and make it a healing and restorative environment.

If we keep in our minds the thought that one day each of us will die, we can **cherish every moment** *that we are alive.*

-Romio Shrestha, Celestial Gallery

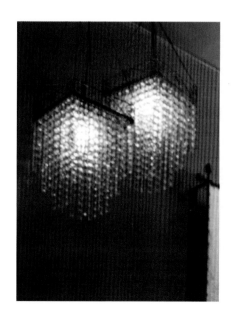

The bathroom can be
        a healing environment,
delightful to the eye
        and the senses that
begins and completes
our restoration each day.

The first step to creating a conscious bathroom is a thorough cleansing and organizing. Clean out all the clutter and dirt from countertops, cabinets and drawers, and throw away everything you don't really use or need. Then you can create a new healing and sensuous environment on a foundation of cleanliness and order.

Also pay special attention to the lighting, in the morning and at night, when you're doing your usual routines. The lighting shouldn't be so dim that you can't see, or so bright that you feel overstimulated or bombarded. You can tell when the lighting works because you'll feel even more refreshed and energized than usual after doing your bathroom routines.

Such basic functional elements as lighting, cabinets, fixtures, mirrors, wallpaper or paint, toilet and tub are the foundation of a bathroom design. The secondary elements are the softer, more personal items where the practical and the sensual meet. These include soft hand and bath towels (preferably organic cotton); rugs; loofahs or scrub brushes; natural scented (or unscented) soaps, shampoos and conditioners; body oils; makeup and more. When it comes to direct contact with your body, natural healthy products promote comfort and health, and enhance your bathroom experience.

Other sensual and visual elements can help turn your bathroom into a temple. Scented candles, incense, essential oils and potpourri can invigorate and revitalize, or soothe and calm, the senses. Potted plants and fresh flowers tend to flourish in a humid bathroom environment, adding beauty and life. Whether small statues or framed pictures, art is always good. A CD player enhances the bathroom ambiance, allowing you to set the mood and tone with your favorite music.

So let your bathroom time be serenity time; let it truly be an altered space that pampers your senses and soothes your soul.

THE MASTER BEDROOM:
YOUR SACRED INNER SANCTUM

IN OUR HECTIC MODERN LIVES AND RAPIDLY CHANGING WORLD, we often neglect to take proper care of ourselves. Our bedrooms should be places of consistent self-care at the highest level. Our bedrooms are our primary nests, literal comfort zones where we spend a third of our lives. The bedroom is the place where, nightly, one seeks rest and rejuvenation for the mind, body and spirit. It is also the place where primary relationships are consummated, nurtured and supported over time. More than any other part of the home, the bedroom should elicit the feeling of ease, as when the heart says "Ahhhh…"

The ideal bedroom design makes us feel as if we are in an elegant and beautiful womb—comfortable, safe and protected, uplifted, pampered and soothed all at the same time. From the moment our feet touch the bedroom carpet on entering, till the time we slide between the sheets at night, every aspect of our bedroom environments should facilitate our final release from the distractions, concerns and anxieties of the day. We should arise each morning refreshed and restored in body, mind and spirit.

Sacred home design is a way of weaving high-level self-care into the physical and spiritual fabric of our homes. And our home environments are often the first places that visibly reveal our lack of self-care. When this happens in your bedroom, the inner sanctum of your sanctuary, you lose precious ground in your restorative environment. Neglecting to make your bed—allowing it, and the bedroom itself, to become cluttered with clothes, books and miscellaneous stuff—is evidence of self-neglect, a sign that you are allowing worldly stresses and concerns to encroach into your mind and spill into your home.

All too often, especially in times of stress, the bedroom is reduced to its baseline functional purpose. It becomes, by default, a place to crash at the end of the day, a de facto hotel room, no longer an altared space. We don't have to allow any room in our houses, or any part of our lives, to lapse into their baseline purposes and functions. That's what "altaring" your space is about.

The bedroom should be the most palpably altared space in one's home. It should be a unique personal environment of total restoration, as exciting, beautiful, sensual and delightful as any five-star hotel room. This is not hyperbole. It is how a sacred bedroom feels, and you can design such a space for yourself. Part of creating a sacred bedroom is visual, and these photographs will stimulate your own creative ideas.

Yet a space is only sacred to the degree that we regard it so, and serve it with sacred intention. This can include such simple rituals as making the bed each morning in a spirit of gratitude; keeping the room clean and conscious; lighting candles or incense; playing soft music; or even chanting, praying, singing and sprinkling water around the room. Our environments reflect and magnify the energy, intention and consciousness we invest in them.

If you really design and serve your bedroom in the ways described and shown here, no other room on the planet, including any hotel room, will nourish you more or surpass your experience at home, which will be your little acre of heaven. Being, sleeping, dreaming or making love in your bedroom will infuse your body, mind and spirit with the healing presence and rejuvenating energy of the sacred. Each day, you will awaken in your sacred bedroom with the feeling of sahej. Your heart will say "Ahhhh…," and you will carry that feeling throughout your day.

THE BED

THE BED IS THE WOMB OF THE HOME, even of one's life. It is, inherently and undeniably, an altared space. We spend more time in bed than in any other single location in life. Most of that time is spent with our eyes closed, in interior states of consciousness different from our waking consciousness. Ostensibly the bed is a place for sleep. Yet we probably experience as wide a range of life lying in bed as we do when we're out in the world. In bed we rest, nap, sleep; talk and make love with our partner or spouse; recover from illness or injury; and lie, often in the dark, pondering a wide range of issues and problems, perhaps solving some of them. Then there are the reveries, and the extraordinary range and phenomena of our dreams that rival and often surpass the realities of our waking life. Many of us meditate and pray in bed. We may even have had profound spiritual experiences in our beds. In a way, one's bed is the closest thing there is in life to a magic carpet.

For all of these reasons, I recommend choosing a bed that delights your eye and lights your fire. Choose a bed that is a worthy support and foundation for your life. Budget low and cut expenses in other areas of your home design if you need to. But let your bed be one place where you don't skimp. Honor yourself and your spouse or partner in this department. Pay attention to each detail of your bed, from the wood frame and headboard, to the mattress you will lie on, to the sheets and blankets that will enfold you.

My wife and I have a large majestic teak bed specially made from a set of antique doors, originally from a Hindu temple. Generations of spiritual seekers and pilgrims passed between these doors that are now the foot- and headboards of our bed. I believe our bed and bedroom are infused with the sacred energy of all that spiritual devotion. It is the

Your home becomes
a living extension of
who you are.
It becomes a temple of
your spirit, a place
of renewal and restoration,
a sanctuary
for your life.

center of our room and, in many ways, the center of our family life. It is the bed on which our daughter was born. It is our magic carpet.

What kind of bed do you deserve to have? My guess is that you will know it when you see it.

CREATING THE SACRED FAMILY BEDROOM

MOST OF US WERE BORN IN BEDS, and some of us in our own homes. My wife and I delivered our daughter at home, in our bedroom, in our bed. Now my wife likes to say that our daughter was "perceived, conceived and delivered" in our bed.

The notion of a family bedroom, and a family bed, may seem odd to those who view the bedroom as a place for romance or sleep. But if you have a very young child or infant, then the concept may not seem strange at all. Love, connection and togetherness are the glue of family relations.

When our children are born, a process of family bonding occurs that deepens and strengthens connections between spouses, as parental partners, and between parents and children. This new phase of family life is an opportunity to develop emotional and spiritual intimacies that will benefit and inform every aspect of our lives.

We may choose to let our infants sleep in cribs in their own rooms, keeping tabs on them at night with baby intercoms. Or, we may choose to put the cribs in our bedrooms or even let the babies sleep with us in our beds. This makes the master bedroom a family bedroom. To create a safe, soft, welcoming space for newborn children, one may create a family nest with plenty of plush pillows and blankets.

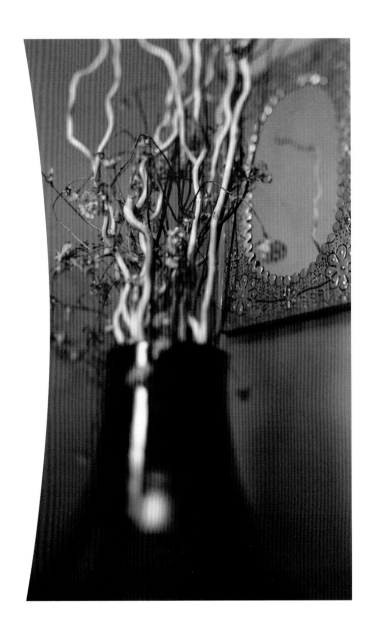

As our children grow, even after they get their own rooms, we can adapt the family bedroom to embrace each phase of their development. Is your toddler already walking and exploring? Consider placing a small upholstered step stool at the side of the bed for easy access. This conveys a welcome message, and also allows the fun and sense of autonomy the young child has in climbing into and off of the bed on his or her own.

A family bedroom adds another dimension to family life. Including our children this way in their earliest and most formative years adds an extra closeness that contributes to their well-being and the family's overall happiness. It will give us cherished memories and give our children the irreplaceable gift of happier, healthier and holier childhoods that will benefit them all their lives.

A client told me she had always wanted a girlish bed that still made her feel safe and protected. So we took this beautiful, simple four-post bed and wrapped it with white chiffon. Now she says that getting into her bed is like entering another world; when she closes the drapes behind her, everything else disappears.

A CHILD'S BEDROOM:
FROM NURTURE AND COMFORT
TO SELF-EXPRESSION AND INDEPENDENCE

ADULT BEDROOM ENVIRONMENTS TEND to remain relatively stable, and once established, design changes are generally nuanced and developmental, rather than dramatic and spontaneous. Once we've created the ideal adult bedroom space, it will likely stay more or less the same for many years.

But children's bedroom designs tend to vary and change, depending on their ages, personalities and interests. Basic needs for quiet, sleep, nurturing and comfort, imagination, play, reading, study, music, independence, self-expression and more will all influence a child's bedroom design as he or she grows through various developmental phases.

Infants are sensually oriented, extremely open to and affected by their environments. The world is an especially stimulating place for the newborn, who hasn't yet learned to filter out numerous impressions. Everything around the baby is new, exciting and at times overwhelming. The reason most infants are asleep more hours than they are awake is because of the overwhelming amount of information and stimuli they take in and process each day. Sleep is when that processing occurs, so it's important that the infant bedroom environment supports this essential need for quiet, rest and sleep.

My wife and I bought our daughter a child-sized Moroccan tent when she was two years old and turned it into an altared space. With her input, we filled it with lots of plush pillows and blankets in soft silk fabrics in soothing and vibrant colors, scented candles (not to burn), pictures of the Sikh gurus and other items, all of her choosing.

Together we created a sacred fort. It may not make the photo shoot for *Better Homes and Gardens*, but it's one of her favorite places in the world to spend time.

Warm, soft lighting and plush, gentle fabrics, pillows and blankets are also important. When it comes to visuals, colorful is good, but don't use too many bright and stimulating colors. Keep a balance of energizing and soothing colors. And when it comes to stuffed animals, toys and pictures for the wall, keep things benign, charming and whimsical, and let your child be part of the selection process.

Because smell is one of the most powerful senses, scent is also important and an anchor for lifelong memories. Always consult your child in choosing scents for his or her bedroom. Age will dictate the manner of response, whether verbal or visceral. Make sure your children really like a scent before it goes into their rooms. Let them smell organic, naturally scented candles, incense, flowers and air fresheners. Which ones do they respond to or reach for? Choose the scents that delight, soothe and calm them. Do a similar test with toys, stuffed animals and wall pictures. As much as possible, and at every age, let your children have a say in what comes into their bedrooms. Their input will make their rooms truly theirs.

As soon as children are able to verbally express their likes and dislikes, they should have direct input regarding the designs of their rooms and the things that go into them. But at every stage of development, the child's bedroom ought to provide a safe and comfortable sanctuary for the body, a nurturing haven for the soul, and a creative and engaging visual and functional environment that matches the imagination, wonder and physicality of the developing body, mind and personality.

THE GUEST BEDROOM:
MI CASA ES SU CASA

MI CASA ES SU CASA, or "My house is your house," is an invitation to guests to feel welcome, appreciated and at home in your home. In virtually all spiritual traditions, guests are honored and served as potential or literal embodiments of the divine. The Old Testament encourages hospitality, even to strangers, as an expression of brotherly love, stating, "...for thereby, some have entertained angels unaware." Why should we regard our own guests as anything less?

The goal of the guest bedroom is to make your guests feel as close to the comfort of their own homes as possible. A guest room should exude welcome, comfort, elegance and charm. It should be your home version of a five-star hotel room for visiting family and friends. The quality of care and attention to detail that goes into designing your guest room makes *welcome* more than just a word. By putting your energy, creativity, spirit and, yes, a little money where your mouth is, you walk your "welcome" talk—and your guests will feel it.

Most guest rooms resemble, by default, a second-rate motel, or a storage space for old or second-hand furniture. You don't have to use top of the line furnishings and materials to create a quality guest room. But quality is important, as is the consciousness and attention you bring to the design process. Remember that a guest bedroom is a part of your temple, and your guests really are embodiments of the divine.

Have you ever traveled and stopped at a hotel, weary after a long day on the road, and checked into a clean, orderly, comfortable and elegant room that was done to a tee, down to the mints on the pillows? Why not extend the same greeting to your guests? But instead of a mint, place a fresh flower on each pillow, something seasonal and softly scented, perhaps a rose, an orange blossom or a jasmine flower.

For an even nicer and more personal touch, create a little altar complete with incense, a candle, a picture or a statue in your guest's spiritual tradition. And to complete the gesture, create a little takeaway gift pouch or basket that expresses your personal appreciation for your guest, perhaps fine candy, your favorite incense and a heartfelt card. Remember, the farewell at parting is as important as the greeting upon arrival.

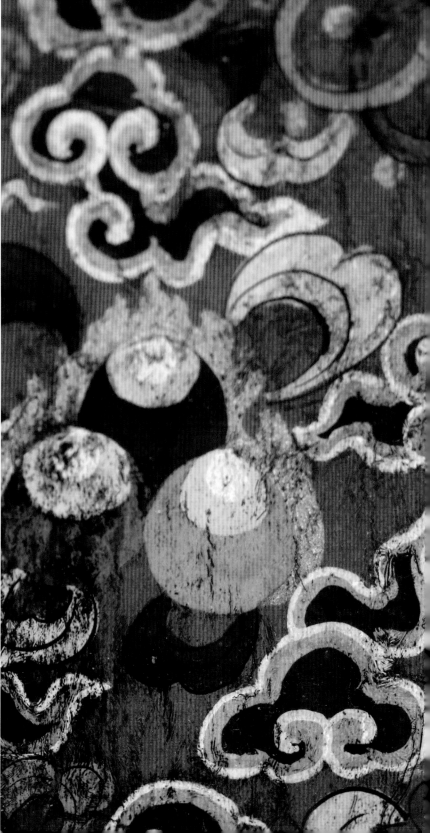

EPILOGUE

OUR SACRED RELATIONSHIP TO HOME

A S NO LIVING ENVIRONMENT IS STATIC, once you complete the formal design of your home, a process will have begun that will last for as long as you live there. Your environment will subtly change, adapt and evolve as you do. It will be enriched by who you are, how you live, and all of the experiences and activities that occur within its walls.

As we grow and settle into our homes, serving them in the simple ways described in this book, we will develop an intimate, appreciative regard for the environments where we find so much calm and comfort, restoration, joy and even grace. And they will shift and adapt to embrace us the way a pair of shoes grows more comfortable and fits better when they are worn in. Our homes will grow around us like a garden, becoming more beautiful, fruitful and mysteriously alive.

From time to time we may notice little gaps and spaces here and there, in different rooms, not as flaws or problems, but as missing pieces in a puzzle that tickle our creativity. We will have little epiphanies and serendipitous discoveries of objects, art, furniture and more that perfectly fit these little gaps, and further enhance and refine our altared spaces. You might say that we are flirting with our houses, and our houses are flirting with us.

As you lovingly and creatively engage with your home environment in this way, you weave your spirit into it. Over time the atmosphere of your home will deepen and become richer, more subtle and satisfying, like fine wine improving with age. It will become infused with your energy, presence and spirit. It will reflect your personality, with all its warmth and depth, its quirks and charms. This is the goal of sacred design. It is what makes your house a home, your home a temple—an altared space that lets your spirit shine.

In your essence, you are already whole, complete and perfect, and you can create a living environment that reflects and supports this.

GRATITUDE

F OR THOSE WITH AN ATTITUDE OF GRATITUDE, the world shall be theirs." So my teacher once said to me. I have so many things to be grateful for.

Each morning I wake to the sounds of silence and go to my meditation room as I have for nearly twenty years. And I am called from my meditation by the sweetest sound known to man, the voice of my daughter Pritam. Returning to the bedroom, I am greeted by the two most graceful, gracious beings God has blessed me with, my wife and daughter, who walk with me on this journey through life.

Many years ago the loving hand of my teacher, Yogi Bhajan, came down upon my back as he called me "Son." Thus began our spiritual journey together. From him I learned that my life's value was in my service and love of those around me, and in the constant remembrance of Wha Hay Guru (in infinite ecstasy I dwell.) Without my teacher, I would have remained the alternative.

My life's journey is a series of reunions with old friends along the way. I am grateful for the many people, clients and friends, who have participated in my life in some significant way, including bringing this book to you. Many of these friends come into my store in Venice out of interest or curiosity, and remain to visit, drink tea, discuss the good and bad of their lives, furnish their homes or simply enjoy the pleasure of good company in a sacred space. The sweet and sacred piece of themselves they leave behind is a part of the living mosaic called Tara Home.

I was truly blessed the day my friend, Siri Darshan, became my partner in Tara Home. Each morning, for almost four years now, I look forward to calling him. Sometimes we speak thirty times a day. I rely on and am supported by his friendship, his intentions and actions. He is for me the embodiment of truthfulness, trustworthiness and integrity. Money has not changed him, and success has made him more humble and gracious. I am also grateful for my "third partner," HG, Siri Darshan's wife. Somehow, and gratefully so, God gave me two partners and my life is better with her in it.

Fourteen years ago, while teaching yoga at a Tony Robbins event in Maui, I met a powerful, gentle, elegant and amazing woman, Jan Miller, who became my friend and my agent extraordinaire for this book. I am blessed to have been able to spend a delightful fraction of time with this special soul over the past fourteen years, even long-distance, one minute at a time.

Years ago, Joely Fisher entered my store leading a boisterous, high-spirited swarm of adults and children. In that first meeting I felt reunited with a long lost friend. Since then, she and her sweet, loving and gracious family have become like members of my own family, and vice versa. I consider her a "holy woman" and I am honored that she wrote the foreword to this book.

This book could not have come into being without the help, support and talents of my friends, brothers and sisters at Mandala Publishing. My gratitude for Raoul Goff, CEO, Lisa Fitzpatrick, Jennifer Gennari, Sonia Vallabh, Nelda Street, Ian Shimkoviak and Alan Hebel. These gracious, passionate and talented members of Mandala have been an inspiration to me, and to countless people around the world who read Mandala's uplifting books.

My gratitude also goes to two wonderful creative people who helped me shape my notes, ideas and jumbled artistic ranting into this beautiful book. Laurel House is an incredibly talented and radiant young woman. Her belief in and work on this book, and the proposal, made it possible. Doug Childers became one of the most important contributors and turned into a great friend and brother

It is your birthright to be
surrounded by beauty,
to know peace and joy,
to live royally and
happily in a sacred home
that elevates your life,
uplifts your spirit,
restores your soul and
connects you
with the flow of love
and prosperity
of the universe.

along the way. An amazing writer, his skill and dedication helped make this book read and feel the way it does. My many thanks and gratitude to Mike Goedecke, my photography partner and mentor. Without his vision of capturing the softness, sweetness and consciousness of a space, this book would be lacking. His eye and the projection of his heart on these pages help make it perfect.

Finally, gratitude for my friend, David Howitt. I have had the honor and pleasure of watching him grow, evolve and develop into a loving servant of others, with passion and a gift for helping individuals and companies fulfill their own potential for serving others. David has been a patron of my photography, my company and my designs, has supported my family, and has been a terrific Godfather for my daughter. I am eternally grateful for his passionate belief and support of me.

I am forty years old and I have had an incredible life filled with love from my family, my friends and strangers. I have traveled around the world and experienced compassion, love and consciousness, and been the recipient of countless blessings from ordinary people who astonish and inspire me and enrich my life. Each day I sit, take a deep breath and feel my connection to the many incredible people who have served me, loved me and given me the experience to write this book for you. Naming them would take too long, and is unnecessary. You would not know them, and their egos do not require such effort.

COLOPHON

PUBLISHER & CREATIVE DIRECTOR: Raoul Goff
EXECUTIVE DIRECTORS: Peter Beren and Michael Madden
ART DIRECTOR: Iain R. Morris
ACQUISITIONS EDITOR: Lisa Fitzpatrick
DESIGNERS: Ian Shimkoviak and Alan Hebel
EDITOR: Doug Childers
MANAGING EDITOR: Jennifer Gennari
ASSISTANT MANAGING EDITOR: Mikayla Butchart
DESIGN SUPERVISOR: Melissa White
PRODUCTION MANAGERS: Noah Potkin and Lina Palma

Mandala would also like to give a very special thank you to Jan Miller,
Annabelle Baxter and Sonia Vallabh for their genuine support, enthusiasm
and goodwill towards making this project a success.